MEN and Relationships

Steven B. Borst

CPH.

SAINT LOUIS

Series editors: Thomas J. Doyle and Rodney L. Rathmann

Write to the Library for the Blind, 1333 S. Kirkwood Road, St. Louis, MO 63122-7295 to obtain this study in braille or large print for the visually impaired.

Copyright © 1996 Concordia Publishing House
3558 South Jefferson Avenue, St. Louis, MO 63118-3968
Manufactured in the United States of America.

CONTENTS

Introduction

The Godly Man Series

In his letter to the recently established Christian church at Philippi, the apostle Paul likened the Christian life to a race. Paul wrote, "Forgetting what is behind and straining toward what is ahead, I press on toward the goal to win the prize for which God has called me heavenward in Christ Jesus" (Philippians 3:13–14).

Each of us who by faith claims Jesus as Lord and Savior has God's permission and His power to forget "what is behind." Over 2,000 years ago, Jesus came to earth, true God, Son of the eternal Father and yet True Man. Conceived by the Holy Spirit and born of the Virgin Mary, Jesus grew as a boy—through childhood and adolescence—to become a mature man. He endured all the temptations and struggles every man has faced and yet committed no sin of thought, word, or action. (See Hebrews 4:14–15.) According to His Father's plan, He suffered and died on the cross as our substitute, taking our sins upon Himself. We can forget our sins because Jesus' love has overcome our past. He has won the victory over our sins and the constraining, handicapping power of the devil. Jesus showed Himself Lord over sin, death, and the devil when He rose from the dead on Easter morning. We who believe in the crucified, risen, and ascended Savior are made new men by the same Holy Spirit who brought us to faith. As God's Spirit gives us new desires and a new set of goals and priorities, He changes us through the Word of God—the Gospel—so that we come to know God's love and the outpouring of His grace in mighty ways, and grow in our relationship with our Father in heaven. Long ago, the psalmist wrote by inspiration of the Holy Spirit the following insight into God and His nature, "His pleasure is not in the strength of the horse, nor His delight in the legs of man; the LORD delights in those who fear Him, who put their hope in His unfailing love" (Psalm 147:10–11).

As we run life's race, our heavenly Father invites us to find our strength and encouragement in Him. His joy is not in any physical means by which men may reach a finish line, such as in the power of a horse or the legs of men. Rather, God finds His joy in those sons who put their hope in Him and in the power of His unfailing love.

God's Word reminds us, "[We] are all sons of God through faith in Christ Jesus" (Galatians 3:26) and our God delights in His relationship with His sons just as every good father prides himself in the growth and accomplishments of his children. He invites us to communicate with Him regularly and often as we experience His Word and respond to His love in prayer.

As we press on toward our heavenly prize, God helps us to live our lives for Him. Many of God's faithful people, both men and women, have lived it before us. Theirs is a heritage for us to build upon and to pass on to those who will follow after us—our wives, children, friends, and others whose lives will be touched by the love and power of God evidenced in our lives.

The writer to the Hebrews encourages us to live as men of faith, reminding us about where to keep our focus as we run life's race: "Therefore, since we are surrounded by such a great cloud of witnesses, let us throw off everything that hinders and the sin that so easily entangles, and let us run with perseverance the race marked out for us. Let us fix our eyes on Jesus, the author and perfecter of our faith, who for the joy set before Him endured the cross, scorning its shame, and sat down at the right hand of the throne of God. Consider Him who endured such opposition from sinful men, so that you will not grow weary and lose heart" (Hebrews 12:1–3).

God's blessings as you run the race and claim the prize already won for you!

About the Godly Man Series

The Godly Man series is especially for men. Written in book-study format, each course in the Godly Man series is organized into chapters suitable for either group or individual study. Periodically throughout each chapter, questions have been provided to further stimulate your thinking, assist you in personal application, and spark group discussion.

How to Use Each Course in the Godly Man Series

Each course in the Godly Man series has been prepared especially for small group settings. It may, however, be used as a self-study or in a traditional Sunday morning Bible class. Chapters of each course may be read in advance of group discussion. Or participants may take turns reading sections of the Bible study during your group study sessions.

Planning for a Small Group Study

1. *Select a leader* for the course or a leader for the day. It will be the leader's responsibility to secure needed materials, to keep the discussion moving, and to help involve all participants.

2. *Emphasize sharing.* Your class will work best if the participants feel comfortable with one another and if all feel their contributions to the class are important and useful. Take the necessary time at the beginning of the course to get to know one another. Since this course deals with relationship issues, you may ask participants to share their names and a little something about a positive relationship they have now or have had in the past. Share what you expect to gain from this course. Develop an atmosphere of openness, trust, and caring among the participants. Agree in advance that private issues shared during your study will remain within the group.

3. *Pray for one another.* Begin and conclude each study session with a prayer. Pray for one another, for your families, your work, and all other aspects of your life. Involve everyone. Consider praying-around-the-circle, with each person offering a specific prayer to God for the person on his left.

As You Plan to Lead the Group

1. Read this guide in its entirety before you lead the first session.

2. Use the Answers and Comments section in the back of the study.

3. Pray each day for those in your group.

4. Depend on the Holy Spirit. Expect His presence; He will guide you and cause you to grow. God will not let His Word return empty (see Isaiah 55:11) as you study it individually or with others in a group.

5. Prepare well, studying each session's material thoroughly. Add your comments in the margins so that you may add your insights to spark conversation and discussion throughout the session.

6. Begin and end the session with prayer.

7. Begin and end on time. Punctuality is a courtesy to everyone and can be a factor to encourage discussion.

8. Find ways to keep the session informal; consider meeting over breakfast at a local restaurant or some other friendly setting where participants can be seated face to face.

9. Keep the class moving. Limit your discussion to questions of interest to the participants. Be selective. You don't need to cover every question. Note that most Bible references are included in the study guide. At times, however, you may want to look up and share additional insights provided by other suggested Bible references.

10. Build one another up through your fellowship and study. Make a conscious effort to support one another in your personal and professional challenges.

Expect and rejoice in God's presence and blessing as He builds your faith and enriches your life through the study of His Word.

Ready

Relationship. From the moment we were born we were in relationship—with the medical team who assisted in our birth, with parents, with grandparents, and with other family members. As you matured, you began to evaluate relationships based upon your feelings, attitudes, and knowledge. List at least 10 relationships you experience now. Then evaluate the relationship using the following code: + = positive relationship; - = negative relationship; 0 = neutral relationship (neither positive nor negative). Now, select 2–3 of the relationships listed and explain how you determined whether it is positive, negative, or neutral. Briefly describe what you have learned through this exercise about your relationships and the means used to evaluate relationships.

Read

Read about the following relationship between a man and his creator.

> **Creator:** I saw the dull yellow eye of the creature open; it breathed hard, and a convulsive motion agitated its limbs. How can I describe my emotions at this catastrophe, or how delineate the wretch whom with such infinite pains and care I had endeavored to form? His yellow skin scarcely covered the work of muscles and arteries beneath;

his teeth of a pearly whiteness; but these luxuriances only formed a more horrid contrast with his watery eyes, that seemed almost of the same color as the dun-white sockets in which they were set, his shriveled complexion and straight black lips. Now that I had finished, the beauty of the dream vanished, and breathless horror and disgust filled my heart. Unable to endure the aspect of the being I had created, I rushed out of the room.

Man: How can I move thee? Will no entreaties cause thee to turn a favorable eye upon thy creature, who implores thy goodness and compassion? Am I not alone, miserably alone? You, my creator, abhor me. Yet it is in your power to recompense me. Let your compassion be moved, and do not disdain me.

Creator: Begone! I will not hear you. There can be no community between you and me; we are enemies.

Fortunately, the above excerpt wasn't taken from the King James Bible! You might have recognized these words as those of Dr. Frankenstein and his monster.

Shelley, Mary, *Frankenstein*. New York: Bantam Books, 1991, pp. 42 and 84.

REACT

1. If you could summarize Frankenstein's view of the being he created with one word, what would it be? Why?

2. What would be a one-word description of how the monster views his creator? Why?

Read

Our relationship with a creator is not a fictional one. We are told in the Bible that we, unlike Frankenstein's monster, were fashioned by a God who made us in His image. After God created man, He wasn't abhorred by what He saw, but "God saw all that He made, and it was very good" (Genesis 1:31).

It didn't take long, however, for man to change. Read what God says about the people He created just five chapters later in Genesis 6:6–7: "The LORD was grieved that He had made man on the earth, and His heart was filled with pain. So the LORD said, 'I will wipe mankind, whom I have created, from the face of the earth ... for I am grieved that I have made them.'"

React

What changed?

What God called "good" after His work of creation, man turned to foul by sin. The verse immediately before God's angry words tells us: "The LORD saw how great man's wickedness on the earth had become, and that every inclination of the thoughts of his heart was only evil all the time" (Genesis 6:5). God's creation had run amuck by rebelling against his Creator. The once perfect creatures had become imperfect and detestable.

1. According to Genesis 6:5, how is our broken relationship with God more than just a matter of some surface sins?

2. Psalm 44:21 tells us that God "knows the secrets of the heart." Consider not only your words and actions, but also your thoughts and intentions this past week. How do you think God would describe your heart?

3. Look back at the one-word description you gave for Dr. Frankenstein. How well could this word work as a description of how God views man in Genesis 6:6–7? Why?

If this were the end of our story, God's words to us would be the same as Frankenstein's to the monster: "Begone! There can be no community between you and me; we are enemies."

Read

God Takes Our Place.

Though it might be hard to imagine, God's Son willingly became a man so that He could take upon Himself the punishment our sins deserved. For 33 years He led a perfect life, and throughout that time, God the Father said of Him, "This is My Son, whom I love; with Him I am well pleased" (Matthew 3:17).

One Friday Jesus was brought to trial and put to death by crucifixion in our place.

React

How does 2 Corinthians 5:21 explain how Jesus acted on our behalf?

To heal our broken relationship with Him, our heavenly Father took all of our vile sin and placed it on His perfect Son. In a very real sense, Jesus became a "monster" for us. He was made grotesque by taking on the sins of the whole world. His death was therefore a fitting punishment indeed! He died to pay for our sin.

The blessing of this event is that God and man can once again have a good relationship. 2 Corinthians 5:21 goes on to tell us exactly that: "so that in Him we might become the righteousness of God." Because Jesus Christ shed His blood as our substitute, we are as pleasing in God's eyes as was Adam at the time of his creation. Through the forgiveness of our sins, we are no longer God's enemies, but instead have been set "right" with God. Through Jesus, God looks upon us and says, "This is very good."

Respond

1. How do you define *relationship*?

2. Webster's Dictionary defines *relationship* as "connection by blood; kinship." In what sense is this especially true concerning our relationship with God?

3. St. Paul says "I resolved to know nothing ... except Jesus Christ and Him crucified." How is Jesus Christ the key to having a healthy relationship with God?

4. Because God responded to our need for a new relationship with Him, we can respond to God with thankfulness and appreciation. By completing the following sentences, you will be able to respond to God's goodness in your own words. After you are done, use the phrases you've written as prayer starters.

When I think about my own sin, my self-esteem sinks because

When I think of You, Jesus, and what You've done for me on the cross, I

God, I know that because of the cross You see me as forgiven and righteous. In Your eyes I am

Thank You, God! Bless my relationship with You. In Jesus' name I pray. Amen.

5. Write 2 Corinthians 5:21 on the top of this week's dayplanner or on the back of a business card. When you are doubting the love of God this week, or are overwhelmed by your sin, read the verse. It's God's promise to you!

Who Am I in Relationship to What I've Got and What I'm Getting?

2

Ready

When was the last time you thought about what you've got and the investment of time and energy it took to get it? The following three tables are meant to give you some sense of that.

In Table A, "Who Am I?" you will inventory your talents and interests. In Table B, "What I've Got," you will inventory seven of your most valuable possessions. In Table C, "What I Hope to Get," you will inventory what you hope to acquire within the next five years.

Table A: Who Am I?

In the Talents and Interests column, list your favorite things to do. Include those things you are especially good at.

In the column labeled with a dollar sign, list how much money you spend per month on each talent or interest. Remember to include all costs associated with this activity (i.e., if a particular interest is a sport, include equipment costs, gas, membership fees, etc.).

In the column labeled with a clock, list how much time you spend per month doing this activity. Remember to include such things as driving time, time to buy supplies, rehearsal/practice time.

In the column labeled with the balance, calculate the total monthly investment for each activity/interest. Investment = cost × time.

Talents & Interests	$	⏰	⚖️

Table A

Table B: What I've Got

In the Possessions column, list the top seven most valuable possessions you have.

In the column labeled with the dollar sign, list how much you spend per month on this item. Remember to include all costs associated with this item, such as insurance and maintenance costs. If the item is paid in full, compute an average monthly cost by dividing its current value by 12 months.

In the column labeled with the clock, list how much time you spend per month using and/or maintaining this item.

In the column labeled with the balance, calculate your total monthly investment. Investment = cost × time.

Possessions	$	🕐	⚖️

Table B

Table C: What I Hope To Get

In the column labeled Future Possessions, list the top three things you hope to acquire in the next five years.

In the column labeled with a dollar sign, list how much you will need to spend per month to acquire this item. Remember to include all costs associated with this item, such as insurance and maintenance costs. If the item will be paid in full, compute an average monthly cost by dividing its purchase price by 12 months.

In the column labeled with a clock, list how much time you estimate spending per month using and/or maintaining this item.

In the column labeled with a balance, calculate your total monthly investment. Investment = cost × time.

Future Possessions	$	🕐	⚖

Table C

Read

Meet Anthony

If you would have asked Anthony to complete the previous exercise, he'd have to consider which part of his life to examine before answering. As a young man, Anthony's inventory list of possessions ran pretty long. His wealthy parents died in his youth, and so Anthony was left with a large estate. His days were filled with leisure, and any work he did was very little and very optional. Young Anthony was living off his inheritance quite comfortably. Life was secure.

That security was shaken one Sunday when he heard the words of Matthew 19:21 read in church: "If you want to be perfect, go, sell your possessions and give to the poor, and you will have treasure in heaven." Anthony felt as if Jesus were speaking directly to him. He struggled with what to do. Should he pretend he hadn't gone to church that day, or should he respond to Jesus' confrontation? Anthony felt he had only one choice: He disposed of all his property and gave the proceeds to the poor.

Anthony moved from a cushy estate to the crude streets within a matter of weeks. In today's society, we would call him homeless. He fled to the desert and lived in a tomb of an abandoned cemetery. He put himself under strict discipline and even gave up food for different lengths of time. By the time Anthony died, only one item remained in his possession column (Table B)—a cloak. He made arrangements that upon his death, it too was to be given to the church.

REACT

WHAT I'VE GOT—IS IT BAD?

The above story is true, and took place in fourth century Egypt. As you might have guessed, Anthony was one of the first Christian monks. Monasticism grew not only out of wanting solitude to study the Bible, but with a conviction that "what I've got" isn't all that good for me.

The Bible records many people who were both poor and rich. On one page we meet a fellow by the name of John the Baptizer who, like Anthony, lived in the desert with only locusts and honey in his pantry. On another page we read about King Solomon. We're told he "was greater in riches and wisdom than all the other kings of the earth" (1 Kings 10:23). Both were considered men of God.

God makes it clear that "what I've got" isn't necessarily bad. Deuteronomy 8:18 tells us: "Remember the LORD your God, for it is He who gives you the ability to produce wealth." In other words, the source of our possessions isn't our ability to acquire them, but God who gave us this ability in the first place.

1. Why does Jesus teach us to pray "give us our daily bread," which includes all our earthly possessions? What does this tell us about God?

2. Joseph of Arimethea was a rich man. The Bible also tells us that he was a disciple of Jesus and the one who bought the tomb in which Jesus was buried. What can we learn from the account of Joseph who, though he had many possessions, remained a faithful servant of Jesus?

Read

When What I've Got Becomes a Problem

Was Anthony right in what he did? If so, does that mean we need to take an eraser to our possessions? Read Matthew 19:21, the verse which so moved Anthony, in its context:

> Now a man came up to Jesus and asked, "Teacher, what good thing must I do to get eternal life?"
>
> "Why do you ask Me about what is good?" Jesus replied. "There is only One who is good. If you want to enter life, obey the commandments."
>
> "Which ones?" the man inquired.
>
> Jesus replied, " 'Do not murder, do not commit adultery, do not steal, do not give false testimony, honor your father and mother,' and 'love your neighbor as yourself.' "
>
> "All these things I have kept," the young man said. "What do I still lack?"
>
> Jesus answered, "If you want to be perfect, go, sell your possessions and give to the poor, and you will have treasure in heaven. Then come, follow Me."
>
> When the young man heard this, he went away sad, because he had great wealth. (Matthew 19:16–22)

REACT

1. What was the attitude of the rich young man in approaching Jesus? Why?

_____honest inquiry

_____cocky

_____trying to get on Jesus' good side

_____naive

_____other

2. What do you think the rich young man was thinking when he told Jesus he'd kept the commandments? Why?

_____"I honestly believe I have kept them."

_____"A couple of mistakes can be overlooked."

_____"I'll tell Jesus what He wants to hear."

_____"I'll lie to look good—hope He doesn't check my references!"

_____Other

3. What was the real reason that the rich young man "went away sad?"

Respond

Jesus' answer to the rich young man's inquiry might have surprised you. After all, it was Jesus who gave up everything for us. He gave up His throne to come to earth. The Ruler of everything became the owner of practically nothing while He lived and taught here. By the time Jesus died, He, like Anthony, had only a cloak in His possession. "Jesus Christ laid down His life for us" (1 John 3:16), and through His death, paid for our sins.

The answer the Bible gives to the question "How do I get eternal life?" is "a man is justified by faith apart from observance of the Law" (Romans 3:28). That's why Jesus' comments are so surprising! Instead of telling the rich young man "believe in Me and you will be saved," Jesus quizzes him about observing the Law and tells him to sell his possessions.

Jesus saw that the problem with the young man wasn't that he was rich, but rather that he loved his possessions more than God. When Jesus quizzed the rich young man regarding the commandments, did you notice that the list of laws Jesus used all dealt with the young man's relationship to other people (murder, adultery, theft, lying)? The only question left to be asked was the question of our last chapter: "Who are you in relationship to God?" That's exactly the question Jesus was getting at when he told the young man to sell all of his possessions. The young man's god was his wealth. He had a First Commandment problem: "You shall have no other gods."

1. How might you cope if you lost all of your possessions in Table B to a natural disaster? Why?

2. Place a check by the items in Tables A, B, and C that most often compete for status as god in people's lives today. Once you've done so, go back and see how high your investment is in these things. Are these things also competing for first priority in your life?

3. The old bumper sticker "He who dies with the most toys wins" has been replaced recently with this one: "He who

dies with the most toys still dies!" How does this slogan emphasize Jesus' point?

Getting a Godly Perspective on What I've Got

Because we are sinful men, it's easy for us to become selfish and to get our priorities mixed up. Conversely, it's not so easy to enjoy the good things which God has given us without becoming proud or spoiled, and without allowing those things to control our lives. Perhaps St. Paul's words on this subject can help us find our way:

> I consider everything a loss compared to the surpassing greatness of knowing Christ Jesus my Lord, for whose sake I have lost all things. I consider them rubbish, that I may gain Christ and be found in Him, not having a righteousness of my own that comes from the law, but that which is through faith in Christ. ... I know what it is to be in need, and I know what it is to have plenty. I have learned the secret of being content in any and every situation, whether well fed or hungry, whether living in plenty or in want. I can do everything through Him who gives me strength. (Philippians 3:8–9, 4:12–13)

1. Take a second look at your items in Table C. Is there something from this column you might delete or add? Why? Has your perspective on acquiring things changed? Why or why not?

2. One way of keeping a healthy perspective of our things is to give a portion of them back to God the Giver. Choose at least one item from Tables A and B that you can give as an offering to serve the Lord.

3. Cut a piece of paper down to the size of a dollar bill. Write the following verse on it and carry it in your wallet. "Godliness with contentment is great gain" (1 Timothy 6:6).

4. In your prayers this week, give thanks to God for Jesus who sacrificed His life so that you might gain what the rich young man was trying to buy, the kingdom of heaven. Take time also to thank Him for each item in your inventory.

Who Am I in Relationship
TO WOMEN?

3

Ready

"Women: Can't live with them; can't live without them."
At least the latter is true. Adam learned quickly that even
living in paradise couldn't make up for the void of female
companionship. God agreed, and after a whole chorus of saying "this is good" in Genesis 1, God looks down at Adam all
alone and says for the first time, "[This] is not good" (Genesis
2:18).

This chapter is devoted to proving wrong the first half of
the sarcastic comment above—men really can have godly relationships with women. Since chapter 5 will have you explore
your relationships to mom and sisters, this chapter will focus
on how you relate to women first as friends and co-workers,
and secondly as wives.

Women as Friends and Co-Workers

Respond to the statements below on the following scale:

1. No way!	2. Probably not	3. Not sure	4. Probably so	5. Absolutely!

After you complete your answers, discuss them with the
group.

☐ It is most natural for women to stay at home.

☐ Women are capable of doing anything they want.

☐ Physically, men are stronger than women.

☐ Emotionally, women are stronger than men.

☐ Men and women are equal.

☐ Men and women think and act differently.

☐ Women are more compassionate than men.

☐ I have no problems giving orders to women.

☐ I have no problems taking orders from women.

☐ Women are meaningfully represented at all levels at my work.

☐ I value a woman's input as much as a man's.

☐ Women like soaps; men like sports.

☐ Women like to talk; men like to act.

☐ Women value relationships; men value accomplishments.

☐ The women I know would be shocked to know that I'm doing this Bible study!

Read

Some people see the Bible as being too ancient to have a healthy view of women. While the oppression of women by men certainly happened during biblical times, a closer look at the Scriptures reveals the dignity which God bestows upon women and the honor and respect He calls men to show to them.

The biblical story of Deborah serves as an excellent example. As you read her account from Judges 4:4–16, circle the different roles Deborah has, and underline those sentences which show Barak's response to Deborah. If you're reading the story out loud in your group, don't get hung up on the pronunciation of some pretty difficult Old Testament names. Just refer to them by their first letter (i.e., Mount Tabor as Mount T).

Deborah, a prophetess, the wife of Lappidoth, was leading Israel at that time. She held court under the Palm of Deborah between Ramah and Bethel in the hill country of Ephraim, and the Israelites came to her to have their disputes decided. She sent for Barak son of Abinoam from Kedesh in Naphtali and said to him, "The LORD, the God of Israel, commands you: 'Go, take with you ten thousand men of Naphtali and Zebulun and lead the way to Mount Tabor. I will lure Sisera, the commander of Jabin's army, with his chariots and his troops to the Kishon River and give him into your hands.' "

Barak said to her, "If you go with me, I will go; but if you don't go with me, I won't go."

"Very well," Deborah said, "I will go with you. But

because of the way you are going about this, the honor will not be yours, for the LORD will hand Sisera over to a woman." So Deborah went with Barak to Kedesh, where he summoned Zebulun and Naphtali. Ten thousand men followed him, and Deborah also went with him.

Now Heber the Kenite had left the other Kenites, the descendants of Hobab, Moses' brother-in-law, and pitched his tent by the great tree in Zaanannim near Kedesh.

When they told Sisera that Barak son of Abinoam had gone up to Mount Tabor, Sisera gathered together his nine hundred iron chariots and all the men with him, from Harosheth Haggoyim to the Kishon River.

Then Deborah said to Barak, "Go! This is the day the Lord has given Sisera into your hands. Has not the LORD gone ahead of you?" So Barak went down Mount Tabor, followed by ten thousand men. At Barak's advance, the LORD routed Sisera and all his chariots and army by the sword, and Sisera abandoned his chariot and fled on foot. But Barak pursued Harsheth Haggoyim. All the troops of Sisera fell by the sword; not a man was left.

REACT

A MODERN WOMAN (AND MAN!)

If you were keeping track of Deborah's roles, you should have circled three of them in the very first verse. Deborah was called to be a prophetess of God, which meant that she was God's spokesperson. She was not only to reveal how God would act in the future, as is the case in our text, but to remind people what God had already revealed: His Law and Gospel. Deborah was also called to be a leader of Israel. The title given to her was "judge," and in this role she settled disputes, guided policy, and even led military campaigns. If these roles weren't enough, we learn finally in verse 4 that Deborah is also a wife. This is a woman with a full plate!

From your underlined verses, you can see how Barak related to such a talented woman. He answered when she summoned, he listened when she spoke, and valued her presence in battle. By being able "to live with" women through mutual respect, Barak shows how you "can't live without them." In his words, "If you don't go with me, I won't go" (v. 8).

1. Identify three women friends or co-workers in your life. How have (or have not) you shown them mutual respect in their talents and roles?

2. Have you ever taken orders from a woman? What was (is) that experience like?

3. What do you think it was like for Lappidoth to be married to such a powerful woman?

4. Open your Bible to Proverbs 31:10–31. Quickly read the numerous roles which the Bible ascribes to women, along with the closing command: "let her works bring her praise" (v. 31).

Read

Jesus and His Women Friends and Co-Workers

The Nicene Creed tells us the primary aim for Jesus' mission: "who for us men and for our salvation came down from heaven." He came first and foremost to save all people from their sins through the payment of His own blood on the cross.

Yet Jesus made it clear that His saving work would produce a by-product in the lives of believers. His followers would be known for their actions prompted by love.

Many of the Jewish leaders saw Jesus more as a revolutionary than a Savior. Christ's life of love often broke societal norms. One example of this is Jesus' disregard for the elaborate Sabbath laws that ruled the weekly lives of the Jews. A further example is how Jesus elevated the dignity of women and involved them in almost every aspect of His ministry.

This type of love and respect shocked not only the men of His day but the women also. The very first contact that Jesus had outside Jewish circles was when He met a Samaritan woman at a well. In the eyes of the Jews, this woman had several strikes against her, not only because she was a Samaritan (an enemy) and a woman but also because she had been divorced five times and was currently living with yet another man. All these facts gave a good Jewish man every reason to disregard and avoid her. Every good Jewish man, that is, except Jesus.

Jesus takes the first step to talk to her and asks her for a drink. He makes it clear that He is even willing to drink from her cup. The woman's response reveals how revolutionary Jesus' actions were: "You are a Jew and I am a Samaritan woman. How can You ask me for a drink? (For Jews do not associate with Samaritans)" (John 4:9). Jesus' response shows His profound respect and love for this woman: "If you knew the gift of God and who it is that asks you for a drink, you would have asked Him and He would have given you living water" (v. 10). Because of His grace, this woman became a Christian convert and one of Jesus' greatest advocates: "Many of the Samaritans from that town believed in Him because of the woman's testimony" (v. 39).

REACT

1. What type of woman epitomizes the Samaritan woman today?

2. How do you think you would react to this woman?

3. How would you have expected Jesus to react to this woman?

4. Women were essential (and faithful) eyewitnesses to Christ's saving work: They were the last to stay by Jesus on the cross and the first to see Jesus risen from the dead. What does this say about the importance of women in Jesus' ministry?

Woman as Wife

Bill and Diane are having marital problems. They have been talking less and less lately, and when they do talk, they tend to argue. With the kids in school, Diane would like to go back to work part-time. Bill doesn't like that idea. Bill would like to buy a larger home. Diane doesn't think they can afford it—especially on one salary. Bill wants more nights at home with the family. Diane wonders why her husband never takes her out anymore. They have grown to distrust one another because they are both strong, opinionated people.

This is Bill and Diane's second counseling session with their pastor. They have been working through some of the frictions mentioned above. This session has uncovered hurt feelings and false expectations for both spouses. As the session closes, Bill throws his hands in the air and remarks, "Pastor, I thought that the Bible tells the wife to submit to her husband. I think that's what's wrong with our marriage. Diane should be less independent and more submissive."

Diane has heard these remarks from Bill before. She rolls her eyes. Their pastor has heard these remarks from dozens of other husbands. He smirks just a bit.

"Bill, you are right that in Ephesians 5:22–24 the wife is asked to submit to her husband in marriage. But have you stopped to think about the type of husband God desires you to be? This would make it a joy for Diane to submit to you out of love. Before our next session, I want you both to read the rest of that chapter and spend some time reflecting on your own behavior and a little less time on each other's."

Read

A Godly Husband

The following verses are Bill and Diane's assignment. As you read them, ask yourself the question, "What kind of husband does God want me to be?"

> Husbands, love your wives, just as Christ loved the church and gave Himself up for her to make her holy, cleansing her by the washing with water through the word, and to present her to Himself as a radiant church, without stain or wrinkle or any other blemish, but holy and blameless. In this same way, husbands ought to love their wives as their own bodies. He who loves his wife loves himself. After all, no one ever hated his own body, but he feeds and cares for it, just as Christ does the church—for we are members of His body. "For this reason a man will leave his father and mother and be united to his wife, and two will become one flesh." This is a profound mystery—but I am talking about Christ and the church. However, each one of you also must love his wife as he loves himself, and the wife must respect her husband. (Ephesians 5:25–33)

Respond

1. Do you love your wife as much as yourself? How do your words and actions show it?

2. In the past month, how have you cared for your wife's needs and desires as if they were your own?

A Profound Mystery

God has pretty lofty expectations for husbands: "Love your wives, just as Christ loved the church." In other words, husbands are to be like Christ to their wives. This type of love isn't just emotional; it's sacrificial.

How much did Christ love His church? He loved her so much that even when she was most rebellious, and downright ugly because of her sin, Jesus Christ "gave Himself up for her to make her holy." What a husband Christ has been to the church, of which Christian husbands are a part! Although He had every right to divorce Himself from us because of our unfaithfulness, Jesus chose the cross to present us to Himself "without stain or wrinkle or any other blemish."

1. For what words and actions toward your wife do you need Christ's forgiveness? For what lack of words and actions? Confess them to Christ, trusting fully in His love and mercy.

2. Identify an area in your relationship with your wife where you need to be more "sacrificial." Make it a goal to work on that area in the coming week.

3. Write your wife a special note tomorrow. Have it read something like this: "Christ loves you so much He died for you. As your husband, I pledge to imitate that love to you. I love you."

Who Am I in Relationship to Work?

4

Ready

Considering the fact that in any given week, most men work as much as they sleep, and work consumes about 30% of our week (or more), the question of who am I in relationship to work is an important one. Take a moment to assess the role of work in your life by filling out the survey below.

Work Survey

Respond to the first 12 statements using the following scale:

1=strongly agree 2=agree 3=not sure 4=disagree 5=strongly disagree

- [ ] 1. I like my work.
- [ ] 2. I am good at what I do.
- [ ] 3. Other people respect the quality of my work.
- [ ] 4. There is a strong connection between my Sunday worship and my Monday work day.
- [ ] 5. The amount of time I work is adversely affecting my other relationships.
- [ ] 6. This bumper sticker slogan describes me: "I owe, I owe, so off to work I go."
- [ ] 7. I could never do anything other than what I'm doing now.
- [ ] 8. God is pleased with what I do for a living.
- [ ] 9. I have a high sense of honesty and integrity at work.
- [ ] 10. I work only as much as I need to get by.
- [ ] 11. I sometimes use work as an excuse to avoid other relationships.
- [ ] 12. Having to work is a curse.

Briefly answer questions 13–16.

13. If you asked me 10 years ago what I would be doing today, I would have said

14. My professional goals are

15. On average, I work _____ hours per week.

16. Ten years from now I'd like to be

Read

Meet the Maglicas

Tony grew up dirt poor in the former Yugoslavia. To be able to escape poverty would be a dream come true. To be able to become one of the most wealthy men in the world would be a total fantasy. Tony Maglica's life is the stuff that fairy tales are made of.

Tony was able to immigrate to one of the only places in

the world where such a fairy tale could take place: the United States. He started his own small business producing flashlights, and was able to make a decent living. During this time he met a woman named Claire and fell in love. The destitution of his former days in Yugoslavia seemed very distant.

Then one day Claire and Tony had an idea (but to this day, they each argue it was their own). Why not expand the flashlight market by updating their product? They worked quickly to jump out of the old paradigm of standard designs, and began to create flashlights that were more sleek and trendy. They went after markets that were up to this time untouched, such as flashlights specifically designed for women, and heavy duty flashlights for police.

Through their efforts, MagLite was born, and it wasn't long before they dominated their competition. By the mid 1990s, their empire was estimated to be worth an unbelievable $300 million. President Bush summarized Tony Maglica's fantastic rise to success this way: "Tony's story is in essence the American Dream." Yet, dreams have a way of being superficial.

It was during this time that Claire and Tony decided to call it quits. Their relationship hadn't been good for a long time, mostly because that relationship, along with almost all of their other personal resources, had been sacrificed to MagLite. Claire says of her work, "It consumed my life. The only thing we talked about was Mag." The children knew this full well also: "Mag instruments is my father's life." Indeed, their father's sentiments were: "I built that business with my blood and sweat."

Picking up the pieces after a divorce is never easy, but for the Maglicas, trying to reconstruct their personal lives has been even more difficult. They were never officially married. Although they were together for 23 years, the state of California does not recognize common-law marriages. MagLite is officially Tony's company, but Claire believes half of the empire should be hers. Early in 1996, a jury awarded $86 million to Claire. Tony, who commented during the course of those proceedings, "I think marriage is a wonderful thing, but I won't let anyone ruin me," is appealing the verdict.

Courtesy of Dateline NBC.

The Consumption Assumption

The altar upon which the Maglicas sacrificed much of their lives is that of the god called capitalism. When capitalism goes from being a sound economic ideology to the foundation for fulfillment, it becomes a deity all its own—a deity that far too many Americans worship and adore. The precepts of this religion identify the U.S. dollar as "almighty," and those who worship it as "consumer." Adherents are indoctrinated that the greenback can give a man the power to do anything he desires.

For the consumer, consumption is the mark of fidelity to this ethic. The more one accesses money, the more he can consume products and services. This, of course, is the basis for fulfillment. Greater consumption is for the consumer the highest moral good, because it is consumption that not only fulfills the self, but fuels the economy.

You have no doubt heard many sermons (though often subtly preached), making consumption a foregone assumption. Credit cards promise you, "We're everywhere you want to be."

Countless advertisements entice you into believing that happiness is only as far away as owning their product. Yet, even when these things are consumed, many people realize that true fulfillment still seems to allude them.

In chapter 2, we established that possessions aren't necessarily bad. The same can be said about consumption. But when a man pledges his allegiance to a life of acquiring, he enters what is known as the "rat race." The only way for most men to acquire more of the deity of the dollar is to work longer hours. Because so many men have bought into the assumption that consumption is the highest good, they continue to sacrifice increasingly the intangible assets of their time, family, and talents to the work place. Like a gerbil running endlessly in a wheel, they work harder and harder to consume more and more, until finally work has consumed them.

While there are many different reasons why men have an unhealthy relationship with their work, the need to consume seems to be the most prevalent. Psalm 39:6 describes this unhealthy relationship like this: "Man is a mere phantom as he goes to and fro: He bustles about, but only in vain; he heaps up wealth, not knowing who will get it."

1. Look back at how you answered questions 4–6, 14, and 15 in the Work Survey. Is capitalism an economic ideology for you or a foundation for fulfillment?

2. Do you have a Maglica story to tell? Have you known someone consumed by their work?

What Kind of Return Are You Getting?

What would you do if you invested your life savings in stocks that were consistently providing a declining return? You'd probably research some other stocks to invest in, and you'd move your money quickly. Think for a moment of your work as your single biggest life investment. What kind of return are you getting for it?

According to Patrick Morley, up to 80% of the workforce doesn't like what they're getting in return for their work. Many men are realizing that even with a hefty monthly paycheck, they lack contentment in what they do. For them, their occupation is a curse that they wish they could sell out as easily as stocks.

From Morley, Patrick M. *The Man in the Mirror*. Nashville: Thomas Nelson, Inc. 1992, p.72.

This type of grind is unfortunate because God meant work to be a gift. After God put in His own six-day work week in which He created the heavens and the earth, "The LORD

God took the man and put him in the Garden of Eden to work it and take care of it" (Genesis 2:15). It was God's purpose that man would look on his work and find satisfaction in it. It was God's desire that man might join with God in saying, "This is good."

1. Look back at how you answered questions 1, 12, and 13 in the Work Survey. What do your answers say about the return you're getting for your work?

2. Consider the chart which follows and comment on how it does or does not describe your experience in the workplace.

Read

God-Pleasing Work

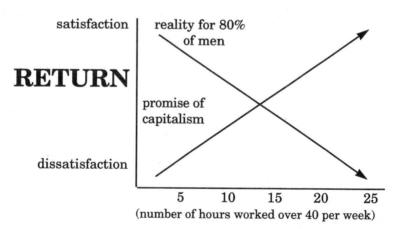

satisfaction

reality for 80% of men

RETURN

promise of capitalism

dissatisfaction

5   10   15   20   25
(number of hours worked over 40 per week)

INVESTMENT

There is a way to get out of the rat race. The Bible would have you consider three important factors as you answer the question "Who am I in relationship to work?"

"Hi, John. I've got someone I'd like you to meet. This is Henry. He's an accountant."

The above introduction has become so commonplace today, that we don't even realize what we are doing. All too often we link our identity directly to our work. What we do becomes who we are. That explains why for some men the loss of identity is a greater devastation than the loss of a paycheck when he becomes unemployed.

For Christian men, such things as identity, purpose, and fulfillment do not find their origin in occupation, but in God. Our loving Father reminds us that our most important calling in life is His calling to us to be His sons. Our identity was forever marked on us at our Baptism, when we were sealed as sons of God by the Holy Spirit. This identity means that in regard to our salvation, we do not need to work! "For it is by grace you have been saved, through faith ... not by works" (Ephesians 2:8–9).

When we find our identity in Christ, then all the other roles we play fall into place. When we see that our primary calling in life is God calling us to be His own, then retirement, disability, or even the devastation of unemployment can't affect who we are. As a matter of fact, we begin to see that God calls His sons into many different roles, such as husband, father, neighbor, and citizen. Our occupation, while important, is only one of these earthly callings.

Factor 2: Integrity

Some men love their work—it's the workplace they can do without! The morality (or lack thereof!) that exists in the work environment can often be a source of temptation, struggle, and dissatisfaction for the Christian man. Whether it is filthy language or downright fraud, the "rules" by which our colleagues (and even our bosses) play are often out of step with what we know to be right.

Steven Covey, in his best-selling book *The 7 Habits of Highly Effective People,* suggests that to be truly successful, you must strive to be ethical. He suggests working "inside-out," which means "to start with the most inside part of self—with your paradigms, your character, and your motives. The inside-out approach says that private victories precede public victories." In other words, what we do flows out of who we are, and true success is measured first and foremost privately, between man and God.

The best-selling book of all time, the Bible, has been teaching us the character ethic for several millennia. It tells us, "Better a little with righteousness than much gain with injustice" (Proverbs 16:8). We see this ethic lived out in one of God's sons; Daniel of the sixth century B.C. Daniel found himself working in a corrupt government and in an environment where his cohorts were jealous of his recent promotion. We're told: "At this, the administrators ... tried to find grounds for charges against Daniel in his conduct of government affairs, but they were unable to do so. They could find no corruption in him, because he was trustworthy and neither corrupt nor negligent" (Daniel 6:4).

Daniel's co-workers finally found a way to undermine him. Daniel was thrown into the lion's den because of his faith. But Daniel had experienced a private victory. By God's grace, he had remained true to who he was, and his work ethic proved that. Ultimately, Daniel experienced public victory as well. God rescued him from the den of lions, and he prospered as the third highest ruler in the kingdom.

Factor 3: In Vocation

Having a sense of vocation flows out of factor 1, having a correct identity. Seeing work as your vocation is sensing that God has equipped you with special talents and has placed you in a particular occupation for a purpose. All Christians have this type of calling, and no one vocation is better than another. Through vocation, God gives dignity to every man, no matter what they do. Martin Luther went so far as to say, "The monastic life [is] no more a state of perfection than the life of a farmer or an artisan. ... All men, whatever their calling, ought to seek perfection, that is, growth in the fear of God, in faith, in the love of their neighbor, and similar spiritual virtues" (*Book of Concord* 275:36–37).

The Christian man who has a high sense of vocation does not merely work for the weekend, as if Monday through Friday were really a waste of time. Rather, it is in his vocation that he is able to serve God and his fellow man. Luther there-fore goes on to say: "Good works should be done because God has commanded them. ... We feel the same way about every work done in the most humble occupation and in private life. Through these works Christ shows His victory ..." (*Book of Concord* 133:189, 192).

Martin Luther's insights tell us that a man's faith, wor-ship, and Bible study are not just things that happen outside the normal routine of life, but instead are things lived out as a man fulfills his vocation. Stated differently, the good works of a Christian man are not only done in sanctuaries, church council meetings, and homeless shelters, but in all that he does to faithfully live out his calling. Therefore, the man who has truly found success and satisfaction in his work is the one who has a real sense of invocation (God's presence) in his voca-tion.

Respond

1. Look back at the following questions in the Work Sur-vey. What did you say regarding the three factors of God-pleasing work in your life?

Identity: Questions 7 and 11

Integrity: Questions 3, 9, and 10

In Vocation: Questions 2, 8, and 16

2. Chuck and James both work as real estate agents in the same office. Chuck is in the rat race. James is a Christian in vocation. How will each of them view the work week ahead?

3. Remember that in the days that lie ahead, you will probably work as much as you sleep, and your work will consume about 30% of your week. What attitudes and actions will you need to adjust to find private victories and true satisfaction in your work?

4. Pray that as the Holy Spirit, working through God's Word, strengthens your faith in Jesus, you may better reflect the three factors of God-pleasing work in your life.

Who Am I in Relationship to Family?

Ready

Being a part of a family means different things for different men. To some it means being a son, to others a brother. To some it means being a husband, and to others a father. Still for others, it means being several or all of the above.

Because we touched on the role of husband in chapter 3, this session will focus on the roles of son, brother, and father. Each member of your group should decide on which role he would like to focus. Divide your group accordingly (no person should be by themselves). Each group should only go through the portion devoted to their chosen role. At the end of the session, your whole group will come back together for a closing exercise.

In Relationship to Family as a Father

Ready

Chuck is a 61-year-old husband and father of four. He is successful and well-respected by those who know him. As he draws near to retirement, he begins to look back at a time when his nest wasn't so empty. He asks himself, "Who was I in relationship to my family?" He does so with some regret.

"There were times when I would leave home with a heavy sigh, knowing that I wasn't spending enough time with my youngest [son]. I would often struggle with the guilt of not being there for him and our other three children ... but pulling away from that dilemma was almost impossible.

"As the demands increased, I asked myself if I had my priorities straight. In the midst of it, I started to do trade-offs. I would say, 'Okay, to make up for all this time, we're going to have a great summer vacation.' But what you forget building up to the vacation is the relationship that needs to be cultivated with your kids. Otherwise, when vacation comes, it's easy to feel this sense of distance. I would ask myself 'Why aren't we closer?' "

"[My kids] were probably hoping I would change, and I say with great sadness today that I wish I had changed more. I regret that I did not make some major changes so I could have spent more time with them."

Chuck Jr. is Chuck's youngest son. Although he is 25 and has now begun his own family, he still feels some pain about growing up. "I felt an increasing amount of emotional bitterness. I felt like I wasn't important enough for Dad to spend time with me. Looking back, I feel like he often chose his work rather than me. It made me very angry. As a teenager, I had a tremendous desire to have a relationship with my father—to help me deal with all the issues and emotions."

There is nothing unique regarding Chuck's family history. What you might find interesting, however, is that the Chuck who made the above confession is the famous author, "sermonator" and pastor, Chuck Swindoll. All too often, many fathers don't ask the question of "Who am I in relationship to my family?" until it's too late—even men of God who serve Him full-time.

Reprinted with permission by *New Man*, Jan/Feb 1996. Strang Communications Co.

React

Reflecting on how well we are doing as fathers is an important exercise. Take a moment to contemplate your fathering, using the chart on the following page. If your child(ren) is/are under 20 years of age, you'll be reviewing the past month, year, and five years. If your child(ren) is/are over 20 years of age, you'll be reviewing the past year, 10 years, and 20 years. Grade yourself on each of the nine important attributes of good fathers on a scale of 1–10. Choose your grade based on the following values. Be honest!

1–3:	Frail Father
4–6:	Functional Father
7–8:	Faithful Father
9–10:	Phenomenal Father

Attribute	Past month/ Past year	Past year/ Past 10 years	Past 5 years/ Past 20 years
1. Supplies for Daily Needs (Psalm 145:15–16)			
2. Gives Protection (Psalm 46:1)			
3. Takes Time to Be There (Psalm 139:7–10)			
4. Is Fair and Impartial (Deuteronomy 32:4)			
5. Is Gracious and Forgiving (Exodus 34:6)			
6. Listens (Psalm 4:3)			
7. Is Patient (2 Peter 3:9)			
8. Is Loving (1 John 4:8)			
9. Is Kind (Psalm 145:9)			
10. Keeps His Promises (2 Timothy 2:13)			

Respond and React

"Healing often starts with a time of forgiveness"

Chuck Jr. and his dad had a breakthrough in their relationship when Chuck Sr. admitted his failures to his son. "Dad came out to Tennessee simply to spend time with me alone. He expressed to me a tremendous amount of sorrow over the lack of time he had spent with me while his ministry was growing and said 'I need you to forgive me.' Those things meant the world to me."

Chuck Swindoll says of that experience, "I believe that when your own weaknesses and blind spots wash over into someone else's life, you owe an apology to the person you've hurt. Healing often starts with a time of forgiveness."

After reviewing your last month, year, and five years, are you in the need of forgiveness for the times you have failed as a father? Swindoll is right! Healing does really begin with forgiveness. There is someone who knows how difficult it can be to be a father and is ready to work that healing in your life. That Father is God, your heavenly Father.

Listen to what the prophet Isaiah says of God: "O LORD, You are our Father. We are the clay, You are the potter; we are all the work of Your hand. Do not be angry beyond measure, O LORD; do not remember our sins forever. Oh, look upon us, we pray, for we are all Your people" (Isaiah 64:8–9). The apostle John tells us that forgiveness for our failing fatherhood has been secured because "the Father has sent His Son to be the Savior of the world" (1 John 4:14).

1. Did you notice that each of the above attributes had a Bible reference next to it? These references aren't demands on what fathers need to do, but rather descriptions of how God is a Father to us. Put a check next to the three fatherly attributes of God which especially give you comfort. Explain why they are so important.

2. You have heard the Good News that through Jesus Christ, our heavenly Father forgives failing and repentant fathers. Are you now willing to ask for that forgiveness from your child(ren)? Write down a specific date to talk to your child(ren). For what will you ask their forgiveness?

It's Not Too Late

Today, Chuck Swindoll is excited as ever at being a father—even with his sons being full grown! By the grace of God, Chuck has this to say about his past and about his future: "There is not a parent alive who won't look back at some point and say, 'Man I wish I'd done such and such.' What's important to remember is that it's never too late to start. It is a conscious effort in my mind that I finish better with my family than I started. I am deliberately pursuing our relationships; I am deliberately calling my sons and daughters, writing them notes, and going after them with passion."

Whether your final score on the above quiz was frail, functional, or even faithful, you are forgiven, loved, and encouraged by your heavenly Father. Your future as a father can be phenomenal. Romans 8:15 tells us, "You did not receive a spirit that makes you a slave again to fear, but you received the Spirit of sonship. And by Him we cry, 'Abba, Father.'"

1. Chuck Swindoll gives two ways in which we can begin to become better fathers. The first is to find a "point of connection" with each one of your children. For one of his sons it was football; for the other it was riding a Harley-Davidson. Brainstorm some points of connection that you can share with your child(ren).

2. A second area to be concerned as a father is this: "Good fathering is about anticipating changes and preparing your family for them. That takes time. And effort—determined effort." For Swindoll, hindsight showed that he should have prepared Chuck Jr. for the marriage of his older brother. This transition meant that Chuck Jr. was not only losing a good friend, but was also becoming the only child left at home. What changes will be happening to your child(ren) over the next year for which you need to prepare them?

You have now completed this section on being in relationship to family as a father. Bring your whole group back together and conclude with the closing exercise at the end of this chapter.

In Relationship to Family as a Son

Ready

Franklin is 44 years old, the son of a very successful father. As he reflects on his life, he does so with the realization that for many years, he was a runaway son who took pleasure in rebellion. He started smoking early on by finding discarded butts and finishing them to the filter. His teenage years saw a fascination for booze, guns, and rock and roll.

His parents tried sending him to a private Christian boarding school, but that had little effect. Franklin admits he was apt to get into fights, and was even known to get the local police after him in high-speed car chases. At age 19, he was expelled from a college in Texas.

Franklin realizes that part of his defiance was due to the pressure of being the son of a successful father. Franklin's father, you see, is Billy Graham.

Respond/React

The Prodigal Goes Home

Two thousand years before Franklin left his family for wild living, and prior to tens of thousands of men who turned prodigal just like him, Jesus taught about the rebelliousness of sons. He told a story about a young man, probably in his early twenties, who took his future inheritance and squandered it on wine and women. After having "seized the day," he found himself homeless and hungry. He was left with only one viable option: to swallow his pride and return to his father. This is what the young man reasoned:

> When he came to his senses, he said, "How many of my father's hired men have food to spare, and here I am starving to death! I will set out and go back to my father and say to him: Father, I have sinned against heaven and against you. I am no longer worthy to be called your son; make me like one of your hired men." So he got up and went to his father. (Luke 15:17–20a)

How is your relationship as a son? Where do you fall on the continuum between prodigy and prodigal? Take a moment to consider what kind of son you've been over the past 10 years (if you're under the age of 25), or over the past 20 years (if you're older than 25). Below are seven scriptural attributes that could be applied to good sons. Grade yourself under each heading on a scale of 1 to 10. Choose your grade based on the following values, and be honest!

1–3:   Sickly Son
4–6:   So-So
7–8:   Successful Son
9–10:   Sensational Son

Attribute	Past month/ Past year	Past year/ Past 10 years	Past 5 years/ Past 20 years
1. Listens to Parents Instructions (John 14:10)			
2. Obeys Parents (Philippians 2:5–8)			
3. Conducts Himself Properly (Hebrews 4:15)			
4. Brings Joy to Parents (Luke 3:22)			
5. Learns fear of the Lord (Luke 2:52)			
6. Attends Worship Regularly (Luke 2:41–49)			
7. Shows Respect for Elders (Matthew 8:14)			

The Prodigal Receives Pardon

The date was July 14, 1974—Franklin's 22d birthday. His evangelist father looked him straight in the eye and spoke plainly: "You can't continue to play the middle ground. Either you're going to choose to follow and obey [Jesus] or reject Him." A few days later, Franklin read Romans 8:1, and found forgiveness: "Therefore, there is now no condemnation for those who are in Christ Jesus." Franklin says that right then and there, "I put my cigarette out and got down on my knees beside my bed. I was His. ... The rebel had found the cause."

This type of life-changing, burden-releasing event took place for the young man in Jesus' lesson too. Listen to the surprise ending of this fractious fellow:

> While he was still a long way off, his father saw him and was filled with compassion for him; he ran to his son, threw his arms around him and kissed him.
>
> The son said to him, "Father, I have sinned against heaven and against you. I am no longer worthy to be called your son."
>
> But the father said to his servants, "Quick! Bring the best robe and put it on him. Put a ring on his finger and sandals on his feet. Bring the fattened calf and kill it. Let's have a feast and celebrate. For this son of mine was dead and is alive again; he was lost and is found." (Luke 15:20b–24)

1. Look back at how you scored yourself in the exercise? In what areas have you failed as a son?

2. What do you think Jesus was trying to teach through this story? Why is the ending so surprising?

3. Through the Gospel, your story as a son can have a surprise ending too. How does Romans 8:1, a verse which meant so much to Franklin Graham, assure you of a favorable homecoming with your heavenly Father?

4. How hard do you think it was for the young man to return home? How hard was it (or will it be!) for you to confess your sins to both your heavenly Father and your earthly parent(s)?

5. Set a specific date to talk to your parent(s), the contents of which could be confession and/or thanksgiving for who they are and what they've done.

A Unique Commandment

Have you ever stopped to think about the Fourth Commandment, "Honor your father and your mother ..."? There are several unique aspects to this commandment which make it different from the rest.

The commandments are broken into two tables or parts. The first table (Commandments 1–3) deals with our relationship with God, such as not having other gods, not using God's name in vain, and remembering to worship. The second table (Commandments 4–10) focuses on our relationships with other people. Honoring your parents is the very first commandment of the second table.

The second unique aspect about this commandment is described for us in Ephesians 6:2–3. " 'Honor your father and mother,'—which is the first commandment with a promise—'that it may go well with you and that you may enjoy long life on the earth.' "

1. Why do you suppose God placed a commandment concerning parents as the very first guideline in relating to other people?

2. What does it mean to "honor" parents? Does this sense of honoring change when a son becomes a man? Can we still honor our parents after they've died?

3. What impact do you suppose God was trying to achieve by attaching a promise to this commandment?

4. How have you seen the promise of Deuteronomy 5:16 kept by God in your life or in the life of someone else in your family?

It's Not Too Late

Perhaps you are suffering from a "Franklin-complex," and feeling a bit overwhelmed at the responsibilities of sonship. Jesus knows what you're going through. He knows what it's like to fulfill the role of a son. John 3:16 says, "God so loved the world that He gave His one and only Son, that whoever believes in Him shall not perish but have eternal life." Jesus is first and foremost the "only-begotten Son" of the Father. But in order to earn our salvation, He also became a son to His mother, Mary, and a stepson to His father, Joseph.

The Bible references next to each of the above attributes aren't further commandments on how to be a good son, but rather descriptions of how Christ perfectly fulfilled His role as Son, both to His heavenly Father and to His earthly parents. This He did for you, so that through faith in Him, you might be seen as a perfect son in the eyes of God. On the cross, all of your sins as a son were exchanged for the perfect obedience that the Son of God and Man achieved for you.

This great exchange truly is good news! Whether you are in your teens or middle-aged, it's never too late to start living in that healing and to start allowing God to empower you to feel a sense of accomplishment as a son.

Next to the numbers below, brainstorm three ways you can bring honor to your parent(s) in the next month.

1.

2.

3.

You have now completed this section on being in relationship to family as a son. Bring your whole group back together and conclude with the closing exercise at the end of this chapter.

In Relationship to Family as a Brother

Ready

Robert and Jay Jamisson are wealthy brothers in Ken Follett's latest novel, *A Place Called Freedom*. As Robert and Jay are introduced early in the book, the reader finds out quickly that there is suspicion, tension, and enmity between these siblings of the 1760s. You would hope that the brothers might have the decency to set such passions aside at special family gatherings. Such is not the case, however, as the clan and their kin gather at Castle Jamisson (located in a small English town called High Glen) on the occasion of Jay's 21st birthday.

Today Father would announce what Jay's portion would be. He knew he was not going to get half, or even a tenth, of his father's fortune. Robert would inherit this estate, with its rich mines, and the fleet of ships he already managed. Jay's mother had counseled him not to argue about that: she knew Father was implacable.

Robert was not merely the only son. He was Father all over again. Jay was different, and that was why his father spurned him. Like Father, Robert was clever, heartless, and mean with money. Jay was easygoing and a spendthrift. Father hated people who were careless with money, especially his money.

• • • •

Don't fight your father, Mother reasoned, but ask for something modest. Younger sons often went out to the colonies: there was a good chance his father would give him the sugar plantation in Barbados, with its estate house and African slaves. Both he and his mother had spoken to his father about it. Sir George had not said yes, but he had not said no, and Jay had high hopes.

• • • •

For a few minutes Jay had forgotten his anxiety, but now it came back with a thump.

• • • •

Sir George led the way out through the main doors. It was dusk. The snow had stopped. "Here," said Sir George. "This is your birthday present."

In front of the house a groom held the most beautiful

horse Jay had ever seen. It was a white stallion about two years old, with the lean lines of an Arab.

* * * *

He was lost in admiration, but his mother's voice cut through his thoughts like a knife. "Is that all?" she said.

* * * *

"Yes," he admitted.

It had not occurred to Jay that this present was being given to him instead of the Barbados property. He stared at his parents as the news sank in. He felt so bitter that he could not speak.

His mother spoke for him.

* * * *

"Robert's getting the castle and the coal mines and the ships and everything else—does he have to have the plantation too?"

"He's the elder son."

* * * *

[The following morning, father Jamisson, his two sons, and two guests prepared to go deer hunting. The dogs were brought out and horses were mounted. Jay did not ride the white stallion given to him the night before.]

Jay stared at his brother, but Robert avoided his eye.

* * * *

He wished he were the only son. He wished Robert were dead. If there were an accident today and Robert was killed, all Jay's troubles would be over.

He wished he had the nerve to kill him. He touched the barrel of the gun slung across his shoulder. He could make it look like an accident. With everyone shooting at the same time, it might be hard to tell who had fired the fatal ball. And even if they guessed the truth, the family would cover it up: nobody wanted scandal.

He felt a thrill of horror that he was even daydreaming about killing Robert. But I would never have had such an idea if Father had treated me fairly, he thought.

* * * *

The hunters spread out, slithering across the sloping mountainside, each looking for a lie from which to take aim.

* * * *

He [Jay] worked his way uphill to a point where a stunted bush broke the skyline, giving him extra cover. ... He could see his stag ... and Robert, below and to Jay's right, twenty-five yards away, an easy target.

His heartbeat seemed to falter as he was struck, yet again, by the thought of killing his brother. The story of Cain and Abel came into his mind. Cain had said, *My punishment is greater than I can bear.* But I feel like that already, Jay thought. I can't bear to be the superfluous second, son, always overlooked, drifting through life with no portion—I just can't bear it.

He tried to push the evil thought out of his mind. He primed his gun.

• • • •

He rolled over and looked across the slope. The deer grazed in peaceful ignorance. ... Then he slowly swung the barrel around until it pointed at Robert's back.

He could say that his elbow slipped on a patch of ice at the crucial moment, causing him to drop his aim to one side and, with tragic ill fortune, shoot his brother in the back. His father might suspect the truth—but he would never be sure, and with only one son left, would he not bury his suspicions and give Jay everything he had previously reserved for Robert?

• • • •

Slowly Jay swung the rifle back until it was pointing at his stag again. Of course he would not kill his brother. It would be unthinkably wicked.

• • • •

He swung the rifle back to Robert.

Father respected strength, decisiveness and ruthlessness. Even if he guessed that the fatal shot was deliberate, he would be forced to realize that Jay was a man, one who could not be ignored or overlooked without dreadful consequences.

• • • •

His whole body was as taut as a harp string, and his muscles began to hurt with the tension, but he did not dare move.

No, he thought, this can't be happening, I'm not going to kill my brother. By God, I will, though, I swear it.

• • • •

The stags froze. Holding his aim on Robert's spine, just between the shoulder blades, Jay squeezed his trigger gently. A bulky form loomed over him and he heard his father shout. ... Just as Jay's gun went off, a booted foot kicked the barrel. It jerked upward, and the ball went harmlessly up into the air. Fear and guilt possessed Jay's heart and he looked up into the enraged face of Sir George.

1. Who is to blame for Jay and Robert's rocky relationship? Why?

____Jay—he's spoiled and selfish.

____Robert—he's "clever, heartless, and mean with money."

____The Mother—she's pampering Jay.

____The Father—he's unfair and exasperating Jay.

2. Do you (or did you) have a rocky relationship with a sibling? Who in your family do you tend to blame for your turmoil?

Where are you at in your relationship as a brother? Take a moment to consider what kind of brother you've been over the past 10 years (if you're under the age of 25), or over the past 20 years (if you're older than 25). Below are six scriptural attributes that could be applied to good brothers. Grade yourself under each heading on a scale of 1 to 10. Choose your grade based on the following values, and be honest!

1–3:   Blundering Brother
4–6:   Battling Brother
7–8:   Admirable Brother
9–10:   Bang-up Brother

Attribute	Past month/ Past year	Past year/ Past 10 years	Past 5 years/ Past 20 years
Supports in Time of Need (Proverbs 17:17)			
Helps Improve and Protect Possessions (Matthew 6:33)			
Comes to Defense of Sibling(s) (Romans 8:33–34)			
Speaks Well of Sibling(s) (Matthew 25:31–34)			
Spends Time with Sibling(s) (Matthew 28:20)			
Loves Sibling(s) Sincerely (John 15:12)			

Ready/React

Oh, Brother!

It's probably not by accident that the Bible spends very little time highlighting positive relationships between a brother and his sibling(s). Instead, we see time after time, the fiction of Jay and Robert come to life in real relationships. The first murder in history was when Cain murdered his brother Abel out of jealousy. Jacob cheated his brother Esau out of his inheritance. Joseph was beaten and sold into slavery by his 10 brothers. If the track record of relationships between children and parents are miserable, the story of siblings, both biblically and today, is downright dismal.

This was even true for Jesus, who also grew up in a family. Not one of His brothers or sisters publicly supported His ministry. As a matter of fact, they had very different ideas about how Jesus should conduct Himself.

"Jesus' brothers said to Him, 'You ought to leave here and go to Judea, so that Your disciples may see the miracles You do. No one who wants to become a public figure acts in secret. Since You are doing these things, show Yourself to the world.' For even His own brothers did not believe in Him" (John 7:3–5).

1. Why do you suppose so many siblings have problems in their relationships?

2. What would it have been like to be Jesus' brother? Do you think you would you have acted differently than they did toward Jesus? Why or why not?

3. Go back and review your scores in the exercise above. In what areas have you bombed as a brother?

BROTHERS CAN FIND BINDING

God does not desire futures filled with bitterness, enmity, and silence. He does not desire this in regard to His relationship with us, or in our relationship with others—especially our brothers and sisters. He alone can offer us hope for healing and for more healthy kinships. What's even more astonishing, however, is that He actually asks sparring siblings to turn to a brother for solutions. Listen to what Hebrews 2:11, 17 says: "Both the one who makes men holy and those who are made holy are of the same family. So Jesus is not ashamed to call them brothers. For this reason He had to be made like His brothers in every way, in order that He might become a merciful and faithful high priest in service to God, and that He might make atonement for the sins of the people."

1. What does it mean to you that Jesus Christ considers you a brother?

2. Hebrews points out that Jesus' greatest act was to "atone for sins." What failures as a man in relationship to his sibling(s) do you need to confess, both to God and to your brothers and sisters?

3. The refrain of a particular communion song states: "And assembled as one, In the name of the Son, Lifting hearts, lifting hands, Celebrating as friends, And proclaiming the Lord, All our praises afford. We are brothers and sisters in Christ." (Dittmer, Terry. "Brothers and Sisters in Christ.") How does God in the Lord's Supper unite all siblings, both spiritual and familial?

4. Building bridges often begins with vulnerability, honesty, and forgiveness. Set a specific date to correspond with a specific sibling.

Being a Better Brother

The power of Christ's death and resurrection has the ability to transform people's lives—especially those of brothers. This was true even in Jesus' own family. After Christ ascended and the early church began, we're told that "they all joined together constantly in prayer, along with the women and Mary the mother of Jesus, and His brothers" (Acts 1:14). Jesus made it a special effort to minister to one particular brother named James. 1 Corinthians 15 tells us that after Jesus rose from the dead, He appeared to "the Twelve" (v. 5), and "to more than 500" eyewitnesses (v. 6) , "then He appeared to James" (v. 7). The love and mercy of the Savior had such an effect on James, that as the early church was being established, we find Jesus' brother as the leader of the church in Jerusalem.

Whether you ranked yourself as a blundering, battling, or even an admirable brother, Christ's atoning work can have the same effect on you. Through the forgiveness won for you by Christ and by His continuing presence in your life, you can begin to do a bang-up job as a brother. "This is how we know what love is: Jesus Christ laid down His life for us. And we ought to lay down our lives for our brothers" (1 John 3:16).

1. Look back at the six attributes of good brothers. Is there one that one of your siblings could especially benefit from right now? Plan a way to implement this attribute.

2. What does it mean to you to "lay down your life" for your brother(s) or sister(s)?

You have now completed this section on being in relationship to family as a brother. Bring your whole group back together and conclude with the closing exercise at the end of this chapter.

Closing Exercise

1. Have one representative from each group share a significant insight they learned about being a father, son, or brother.

2. Have one representative from each group share how God has significant insight in being a father, son, or brother. Focus especially on how Jesus Christ is central in bringing healing and empowerment to these roles.

3. As a devotion this week, do one of the following:

* look up the Bible verses behind each one of the attributes in the role that you studied; or

* work through one of the other studies in this chapter. Consider going through it with your child(ren), parent(s), or sibling(s).

4. Close by praying together: "Heavenly Father, we implore You to visit our homes. Keep far from us all harm and danger. Allow us to live together in peace under the protection of Your holy angels, and may Your blessing be with us forever. We pray this in the name of Jesus Christ, Your Son, our Brother. Amen." (Based on prayer from *Lutheran Worship,* p. 129.)

Who Am I in Relationship TO Leisure?

6

Ready

In the space below, draw your ideal picture of leisure. Your picture could reflect weekly leisure activities or perhaps your dream vacation. You may use symbols in your drawing but not words. After you're done, share your picture with the rest of the group. Be creative!

Read

What the Question Is Not

In many parts of the country, you can go out to eat at a restaurant called "T. G. I. Friday's." At first glance, this name seems a bit odd. Do they only want our patronage on Fridays? When you think about it, however, you realize that this restaurant chain has captured a need that every human desires—free time. If you can associate leisure, fun, and play with their restaurant, then who wouldn't want to go there to eat—even if it is only "humpday."

In this devotional series, you have considered some pretty important relationships. Men need to consider their relationship to God, family, work, and wages. Have you ever stopped to consider that taking free time is one of your important responsibilities as well?

Jesus knew that to take time for rest and leisure wasn't a question at all. He worked hard during His public ministry and was still hounded by people who needed Him. Yet He knew the need for taking a break. On one particular day, He had been teaching thousands of people and healing the sick all day long. As night came, He took a boy's sack lunch, multiplied it, and fed the people fish and bread so they wouldn't go hungry. Listen to what happens right after this dinner miracle:

> Immediately Jesus made the disciples get into the boat and go on ahead of Him to the other side, while He dismissed the crowd. After He had dismissed them, He went up into the hills by Himself to pray. When evening came, He was there alone. (Matthew 14:22–23)

REACT

1. Check the box which best describes your leisure time.
_____With all my responsibilities, who's got time for leisure.
_____I am inconsistent in taking time out for myself.
_____Leisure activities are a scheduled part of my week.
_____Other
2. How hard do you think it was for Jesus to turn people away when He needed rest?

3. How good or bad are you at protecting your free time?

Read

What the Question Is

Several years ago, the Red Sox's Wade Boggs was one of the hottest players in baseball. His bat seemed as if it could hit anything thrown at him, and he eventually went on to win the American League batting title. Many Bostonians had pinned their hopes on Wade for a division pennant, but Boggs and company were unable to deliver the championship to "Beantown."

It was during this time, when the spotlight on Boggs was as hot as his bat, that Wade made a very public confession—he was addicted to sex. For the first time this type of addiction was talked about in public. Boggs said that he turned to sex with countless women as an escape from the demands of his career. Many fans who knew little if anything about this addiction wondered if there was anything that human beings wouldn't abuse.

You don't need to look far to see that too many people abuse their free time. Things that are meant to enhance leisure, such as alcohol or sports, have become addictions. Desperate to find greater highs, many people have turned to harder and harder drugs to escape. The most pertinent question facing men today is not "Should you set aside free time?" Instead, a more important question is "How are you using your free time?"

React

1. Sin has marred every good and perfect gift of God, including our sexuality. Can you think of other good and perfect gifts of God that have been abused or misused?

2. In what free-time activities are you involved? How do you use this free time?

Read

What the Answer Is

We all know what it's like to put in too many long days at work without a break. We become more easily fatigued, our eating habits go from not so good to worse, and it takes us longer to complete tasks that seem easier when we are rested. It is during those times that we become most aware of our need for a break. We feel overworked and drained, and we know that if we could just get some time to "sharpen our saw" or "get juiced up," we could be more efficient.

Even though we probably haven't realized it, the answer to our needs lies in the word recreation. True recreation "re-creates" a person so that they might more fully accomplish the other responsibilities in their life. When we don't use, wrongly choose, or misuse our leisure activities, the end result is not re-creation, but further deterioration.

Herein lies the answer to the question of our chapter: "Who am I in relationship to leisure?" Men who have a healthy relationship with leisure aren't ruled by their activities and aren't prone to abusing them. As we work toward this healthy relationship, we are actively to seek those activities which will serve us. These activities will be things that we enjoy and which will offer us true re-creation. It is then that we will see our free time not as an option but as a responsibility.

Respond

1. Make a list of five leisure activities which you have participated in over the past week. In the blank next to them,

rank the amount of "re-creating" you received on a scale of 1 to 10 (with 10 being the highest form of re-creation).

_____1.

_____2.

_____3.

_____4.

_____5.

2. Watching television is a leisure activity many people abuse. How many hours a day do you watch TV? Are these hours superseding other quality free-time activities?

3. Is it possible to make free time too much of a priority? If so, give an example.

Read

Does God Need to Rest?

It's not at all surprising that as soon as God was done creating, He made provisions for re-creating. Read the following verses from the second chapter of Genesis.

> The heavens and the earth were completed in all their vast array. By the seventh day God had finished the work He had been doing; so on the seventh day He rested from all His work. And God blessed the seventh day and made it holy, because on it He rested from all the work of creating that He had done. (Genesis 2:1–3)

This might cause us to wonder: If God is all powerful,

then why did He need to take a day off? Sure, creating the whole universe in just six days is anyone's definition of a difficult work week, but did all that creating really wear Him out?

For God, rest isn't just lying around. He stopped working to enjoy the fruit of His work. ("God saw all that He had made, and it was very good.") In other words, God's idea of rest is spending time with us. The God who created us desires to re-create us on a regular basis through His presence. He created us in a way that we actually yearn for this time with Him.

Where can we find this holy rest? We get a taste of it during the week when we pray or spend time in God's Word. But the climax of this holy rest comes during worship; typically on Sunday. In worship, you will find relief from the heavy burden of your sins through absolution (forgiveness). During the Lord's Supper, Christ will take time to be with you and will offer you His very body and blood to make you holy. In worship, God "rests" with us, and therefore offers us the greatest form of re-creation. If you're less than satisfied with the re-creation you have been getting from your other leisure activities, perhaps it's because you've been neglecting to rest with God in worship. It is this re-creation that permeates and gives satisfaction to all our other leisure activities.

1. On Sunday mornings, many men try to fill their yearning for rest through enjoying the comics, drinking a cup of coffee, or watching football. While all these activities do offer some form of relaxation, how do they fall short of true re-creation?

2. When and if we go to church begrudgingly, what are we likely to miss out on?

3. Jesus said, "Come unto Me, all you who are heavy-laden, and I will give you rest." How can "holy rest" only be found in the Holy One?

4. Look back at your "picture of leisure." How does it fit in with what you've learned in this chapter?

5. In the space below, draw a second picture of leisure. This time, have it reflect the re-creation God desires to give you in worship. After you're done, take both pictures home with you and tape them in a prominent place. Use them as reminders for getting some quality rest that includes a healthy dose of recreation this week.

Answers and Comments

1

Who Am I in Relationship to God?

Opening

Pray together that the Lord would bless your study of God's Word.

Ready

Have participants complete the activity suggested in this section. Invite volunteers to share what they learned through the activity about their relationships. Answers will vary.

Read

Read the excerpts from *Frankenstein.*

React

Discuss the questions.

1. Answers will vary. Some of the possible responses might be "disgust" and "hate". The creator is extremely disappointed in the result of his creative efforts.

2. The monster views the creator as one who despises him. The monster implores the creator's compassion and love.

Read

Read about God as Creator and His relationship with the created.

React

Discuss the question included in this section.

1. Man's wickedness was great, including the very inclination of his heart.

2. Answers will vary. No doubt some of our thoughts and actions have been inclined toward evil.

3. God loves man. He grieves that His creature has become so evil.

Read

Read aloud this section that describes how God's Son, Jesus Christ, came to earth to suffer and die for the sins of His creation.

React

God made His only Son, who had no sin, to be a sin for us so that through Him we might receive God's righteousness. (See 2 Corinthians 5:21.)

Respond

1. Answers will vary.

2. Through Jesus we have a relationship to God—a "connection by blood" through faith in Him. Jesus' blood shed on the cross accomplished that which we were unable to do on our own—forgiveness of sins and eternal life.

3. We have a healthy relationship with God only through faith in Jesus Christ. Jesus restored the broken relationship that existed between God and man because of sin.

4. Answers will vary.

5. Urge participants to write 2 Corinthians 5:21 where they will see it often during the coming week.

Closing

Invite participants to share concerns, joys, and sorrows that they wish to share with God in prayer. Then if participants feel comfortable doing so, invite them to pray for these concerns. Close the prayer by thanking God for the relationship He restored between Him and us through His Son's death on the cross.

2

Who Am I in Relationship to What I've Got and What I'm Getting?

Opening

Pray that the Holy Spirit would work mightily as you study God's Word today so that you might receive wisdom from God concerning the priorities in your life.

Ready

Invite participants to complete the first table. Ask volunteers to share what they learned from completing the first table. Then have participants complete the "What I've Got" table. Ask volunteers to share their monthly investment. Then have participants complete Table C. Invite volunteers to share their monthly investment in what they hope to get.

Read

MEET ANTHONY

Read the story of Anthony.

React

WHAT I'VE GOT—IS IT BAD?

1. God desires to give us all that we need to sustain the life He has given to us. He loves us.

2. Answers will vary. God blesses some with great riches. Wealth is only evil when it becomes the first and foremost priority in our lives. God desires to be number 1 in our lives.

Read

WHEN WHAT I'VE GOT BECOMES A PROBLEM

Read the story of the rich young man.

REACT

1. Any of the responses may be true. What is certain is that the man rejected that which Jesus desired to give him. Answers will vary.

2. The man believed he had done a very good job in trying to keep the commandments. People today may also delude themselves into thinking that because they try to be good people, God will love them. We know from Scripture that anything we do in order to try to earn God's favor is worthless. Forgiveness of sins and eternal life are gifts from God.

3. The rich young man went away sad because he rejected that which he must do in order to make God number 1 in his life. As he walked away from Jesus, he was walking away from the love and forgiveness God in Christ wanted to provide for him.

RESPOND

1. Answers will vary.

2. Urge participants to be honest in responding to this question.

3. Anyone whose hope for the future rests in what they can acquire or accumulate will find only death. Those whose hope for the future rests in Jesus Christ alone will receive the gift of eternal life.

GETTING A GODLY PERSPECTIVE ON WHAT I'VE GOT

1. Answers will vary.

2. Answers will vary.

3. Urge participants to write 1 Timothy 6:6 on a dollar-bill sized sheet of paper to put in their wallet.

4. Urge participants to remember the blessings God has provided to them in their prayers.

CLOSING

Use the prayer suggestion in number 4 as the basis for your closing prayer.

3

Who Am I in Relationship to Women?

Opening

Pray that the Lord would richly bless your study of His Word today.

Ready

Read aloud this opening section.

Women as Friends and Co-Workers

Respond to the statements using the suggested scale. When most participants have completed the activity, invite volunteers to share their responses.

Read

Read about Deborah, one of God's faithful servants.

React

A Modern Woman (and Man!)

Review with participants the roles Deborah took on in service to God and the people of Israel.

1. Answers will vary. Invite volunteers to share.
2. Answers will vary.
3. Answers will vary.
4. A wife is noble, worth far more than rubies, provides for her family, works vigorously, etc.

Read

Jesus and His Women Friends and Co-Workers

Read about the acceptance and love Jesus demonstrated to women.

React

1. Women who are prostitutes epitomize the Samaritan woman today.

2. Answers will vary.

3. Jesus demonstrates love and acceptance to all people, including those people would consider the worst of sinners.

4. Women were extremely important to Jesus' ministry.

Woman as Wife

Read about the marital problems of Bill and Diane.

Read

A Godly Husband

Read aloud Ephesians 5:22–33.

Respond

1. Answers will vary.

2. Again, answers will vary. Urge volunteers to share their responses honestly.

A Profound Mystery

Read aloud God's expectations for husbands.

1. Answers will vary.

2. Urge participants to identify an area in their relationship with their wives where they can be more sacrificial.

3. Urge participants to write the special note to their wives.

Close

Invite participants to share needs, concerns, joys, and sorrows that they would like to bring before the Lord's throne in prayer. Ask for volunteers to pray.

4

Who Am I in Relationship to Work?

Opening

Pray that the Lord would bless your study together today as you explore what God says about work.

Ready

Read aloud the introductory paragraph.

Work Survey

Urge participants to complete the work survey independently. Then invite volunteers to share how they responded.

Discuss the questions that follow the survey.

13–16. Answers will vary.

Read

Meet the Maglicas

Read aloud or silently the story of the Maglica family.

React

The Consumption Assumption

1. Urge participants to answer the question honestly. Answers will vary.

2. Answers will vary.

What Kind of Return Are You Getting?

1. Answers will vary.

2. Allow participants time to share what kind of return on their investment they receive from their work.

Read

God-pleasing Work

Discuss the three important factors to consider when answering the question "Who am I in relationship to work?"

Respond

1. Answers will vary.

2. Work has become for Chuck his number 1 priority and concern. For James work is a means to an end. God remains his number 1 priority. James serves God through his work.

3. Answers will vary.

4. Use the prayer suggestion as the closing prayer.

Closing

Use the prayer suggestion in number 4.

5

Who Am I in Relationship to Family?

Opening

Pray that the Holy Spirit would bless your study of God's Word today.

Ready

Read the introductory paragraphs. You may wish to divide the study group into small groups as suggested. Or, if time permits, you may wish to study all of the sections.

In Relationship to Family as a Father

Ready

Read the story of Chuck Swindoll and his relationship to his son.

React

Invite participants to grade themselves as fathers. Read aloud the suggested Bible passages next to each attribute. Discuss briefly each of the attributes.

Respond and React

1. Answers will vary.
2. Invite participants to confess honestly their failings as fathers. Assure participants of the forgiveness Jesus won for each of them when He suffered and died on the cross.

It's Not Too Late

1. Urge participants to brainstorm some possible points of connection that they can share with their children.
2. Discuss changes that will be occurring in their children's lives over the next few years. Ask, "How will you respond to these changes? Why is it important to respond to each of these changes in appropriate ways?"

In Relationship to Family as a Son

Ready

Read aloud the story of Franklin.

Respond/React

The Prodigal Goes Home

After reading the introductory paragraphs, have participants grade themselves as sons. Read aloud and briefly discuss each of the Bible references next to the attributes.

The Prodigal Receives Pardon

Read aloud the story of reconciliation between the father and the prodigal son.

1. Answers will vary.

2. Using the parable of the prodigal son, Jesus taught about the unconditional love God has for all sinners. The ending to the parable is surprising because of the great love the father demonstrates to his wayward son. Our human nature might cause us to respond to a wayward child with vengeance or anger. The love of God in Christ Jesus motivates us to demonstrate His love in our relationship with others.

3. "There is now no condemnation for those who are in Christ Jesus." God accepts us unconditionally by His grace through faith in Christ Jesus.

4. Answers will vary. God invites us to confess our sin to Him and to receive the gift of forgiveness of sins through faith in Christ Jesus.

5. Urge participants to complete this activity.

A Unique Commandment

Read the introductory paragraphs about the Fourth Commandment.

1. Our relationship with our parents sets the stage for all other relationships. God desires that we honor our parents.

2. Honor is a deep respect and love. A son or daughter can continue to honor his or her parents even when they are grown. We continue to love and to respect deeply our parents even after they have died.

3. God emphasizes the importance of this commandment

by attaching to it a promise. God knows what is best for us. A child who honors his parent will experience blessings in relationships. Parents are given to us as blessings from God—God provides them wisdom that they share with us.

4. Answers will vary.

It's Not Too Late

1–3. Have participants brainstorm ways they can bring honor to their parents. Answers will vary.

In Relationship to Family as a Brother

Ready

Read aloud and discuss the story of Robert and Jay Jamisson.

1. Answers will vary. Usually in a stormy relationship, more than one person is to blame.

2. Answers will vary.

Urge participants to grade themselves using the scriptural attributes included in the chart. Have volunteers read aloud the scriptural references.

Ready/React

Oh, Brother!

Read aloud the introductory paragraphs.

1. Because of sin, many siblings have problems in their relationships.

2. Answers will vary.

3. Invite volunteers to confess their sinful thoughts, words, or deeds committed against their sibling(s).

Brothers Can Find Binding

1. Because Jesus Christ accepts us as His brother, we through faith can call God our Father. Jesus has reconciled the relationship destroyed by sin between God and us and between us and others.

2. Answers will vary.

3. Through faith all who receive the body and the blood of Jesus Christ in the Lord's Supper are united as brothers and sisters.

4. Urge participants to complete the suggested activity.

BEING A BETTER BROTHER

1. Answers will vary.

2. To "lay down your life" means you sacrificially love your brother. You love your brother more than you love yourself.

Closing Exercise

1. Answers will vary. Urge participants to share openly and honestly.

2. Answers will vary.

3. Urge participants to complete the devotional suggestions.

4. Use the prayer as the closing worship activity.

Closing

Pray the prayer printed in number 4.

6

Who Am I in Relationship to Leisure?

Opening

Pray that the Holy Spirit would provide you wisdom concerning leisure and your use of leisure as you study God's Word today.

Ready

Urge participants to draw their ideal picture of leisure in the space provided. After most participants have completed the activity, invite volunteers to share their drawings with the rest of the group.

Read

What the Question Is Not

Read aloud these introductory paragraphs.

React

1. Answers will vary.
2. Jesus eagerly invited all to come to Him. Jesus did not turn people away from Him.
3. Answers will vary.

Read

What the Question Is

Read the story of Wade Boggs.

React

1. All good and perfect gifts of God have been abused or misused because of sin. Some of these include television, technology, radio, sexuality, alcohol, food, etc.
2. Answers will vary.

Read

Wʜᴀᴛ ᴛʜᴇ Aɴsᴡᴇʀ Is

Read aloud this section that emphasizes how recreation is re-creation.

Respond

1. Urge participants to complete this activity. Answers will vary.

2. Again, answers will vary. Urge participants to answer the question honestly.

3. Anything that becomes number 1 in our lives other than God is sinful. When leisure becomes our number 1 priority, it can become a god to us.

Read

Doᴇs God Nᴇᴇᴅ ᴛo Rᴇsᴛ

Read aloud this review of the creation account.

1. True re-creation only comes through faith strengthened by the power of the Holy Spirit working through the Gospel.

2. God invites us all to come to Him. When we do not desire the faith-strengthening power God offers through His Word, we are likely to ignore or to refuse to listen to what He has to say. God can melt even the coldest and most hardened hearts by the power of the Holy Spirit working through God's Word.

3. Holy rest can only be found in the person and work of Jesus Christ. The Gospel provides us spiritual rest for through it we receive the promise of life eternal.

4. Answers will vary.

5. Urge participants to complete and then share their second picture of leisure. Ask, "How is this second picture different than your first picture?"

Closing

Invite participants to share prayer requests. Then appoint a leader to pray or take turns praying for the needs and concerns that have been raised.